The Councillor's Handbook
1987 Edition

Cliff Davis-Coleman BA(Hons)

published by
Municipal Journal Limited
178-202 Great Portland Street London W1N 6NH
Tel: 01-637 2400 Fax: 01-631 0360
Price: £2.00 including postage and packing

ISBN 0 900 552 48 4
© Municipal Journal Limited.

CONTENTS

EDITOR'S INTRODUCTION

This handbook is primarily intended for the newly-elected councillor but will prove useful to more experienced members and for officers. It updates previous Handbooks taking into account the various changes which have occurred in local government as a result of central government legislation.

I hope it proves helpful. Local government can be a complex business and a little help in the initial stages for new members will hopefully provide dividends.

I should like to thank Cliff Davis-Coleman for undertaking the task of virtually rewriting the previous Handbook. Thanks are also due to the Department of the Environment, Tony Page, Robin Wendt, Chief Executive of Cheshire County Council for permission to reproduce his county's Standing Orders in the appendices, and David Lunn, Borough Secretary, Royal Borough of Windsor and Maidenhead DC, for his invaluable advice on the Handbook's legal aspects.

John Jackson
Editor
Municipal Journal

PREFACE

As an elected member you will already know – or you may be about to learn – that the workload imposed upon the modern councillor is substantial. Be you a backbencher or a committee chairman, the mass of reports that will be falling through your letterbox, the journals that will be pushed your way and the circulars from Government departments that have to be heeded can have the effect of dampening the enthusiasm that surrounded your original election. This handbook is intended to be used in two ways. It will attempt to put the role of the local councillor into context with the national local government scene, and serve as a useful – if brief – index to the workings of the council. In addition the appendices contain an A to Z of local government which will help you unravel the jargon that envelopes the local authority world.

We must, however, stress the importance of drawing upon every resource available to the councillor. Primary among these are the services of the Chief Executive and his staff. The officers are there to run the administration, implement council policy and, above all, serve the elected representatives of the local populace. Throughout this handbook reference will be made to Acts of Parliament, representative bodies and statutory bodies. Brief descriptions of their content and function will be contained in these pages but for a fuller explanation, the advice of your officers should always be sought.

INTRODUCTION

The history of modern local government can be traced back to the late 1800s. Cllr Joseph Chamberlain, mayor of the Birmingham Corporation between 1873 and 1876, is accepted as the architect not only of service provision and the local authority, but also for establishing the role of the professional local government officer.

His vision of a slum-free city with adequate supplies of housing, water, power and social services is one that has transcended the years, but it has also become the focus of friction between central and local government.

People seek public office for a variety of reasons. The desire to provide a service to the local community is high on every candidate's agenda, but the influence of the political parties on the local scene has tended to diminish the number of independent candidates. Even within the confines of a political party there remain the ward and single issue councillors — those who become councillors for example to fight the corner for the disabled or other minority groups. Increasingly, the town hall is being used as a platform from which to launch a national political career and it is perhaps this more than any other factor that has placed local government, in media terms, on a par with national political considerations.

The influence of politics in the local context has also given rise to a plethora of legislation. Never before have local authorities been subject to such Parliamentary attention.

Bearing this in mind, it is important for a new councillor or an experienced councillor for that matter to keep abreast of events in the national and local scene. The Municipal Group's *Digest of New Legislation* provides quick easy-to-read updates of Acts of Parliament which are published as relevant local government legislation passes onto the Statute Book. Other sources of information include the local government and national press. No longer can a local councillor afford to view himself or herself in a purely local context.

STRUCTURES

The abolition of the Greater London Council and the six metropolitan county councils (Greater Manchester, Merseyside, South Yorkshire, Tyne and Wear, West Midlands and West Yorkshire) was the most fundamental change in the structure of local government since the reorganisation of April 1974.

The **Local Government Act 1972** marked the end of the all-purpose county borough. In their place, the Act created 39 non-metropolitan county authorities and 296 non-metropolitan districts. The Greater London Council had been in place since 1964, along with the 32 London boroughs and the City of London Corporation, but the 1974 Act introduced the six metropolitan county councils which were latterly abolished in 1986.

Although the title 'county borough' disappeared, districts are still permitted to petition for borough status. Parishes survived the reorganisation, and the Act made allowance for the creation of urban parishes.

In **Wales**, the number of counties was reduced to eight. There are 37 district councils and instead of parishes the Province has community councils whose functions are broadly similar to those of their English counterparts. The functions of the respective tiers can be broken down as follows:

SCOTLAND
DISTRICT COUNCILS: Planning, environmental health, housing, parks and recreation, libraries, museums and art galleries, swimming baths and licensing of entertainment and gambling etc.

REGIONAL COUNCILS: Education, social work, roads and transport, general planning, water and sewerage services, police and fire services, consumer protection, coastal protection, valuation and rating.

ENGLAND & WALES
COUNTY COUNCILS: Education, Personal Social Services, Libraries, Museums and Art Galleries, Highways, Parking, Structure Plans, National Parks, Mineral and Gravel Extraction, Refuse Disposal, Consumer Protection Services, Police and Fire Services, plus residual housing powers.

SHIRE DISTRICTS: Housing, Public Health, Markets, Refuse Collection, Local Plans and Development Control, Licensing and Land Charges, Footpaths, Cemetaries, Swimming Baths, Parks, Open Spaces, Allotments, Car Parks and Entertainment. In **Wales** only, districts are also responsible for refuse disposal.

PARISHES: In many areas parishes have concurrent powers with districts in areas such as street lighting, footpaths and car parks. However, their main areas of activity are lighting, recreation grounds and allotments.

NB: In many parts of the country, district councils operate some of the county council functions, notably traffic management and highway maintenance, on an agency basis withing their areas. Similarly, many districts have agency arrangements with the water authorities to enable them to undertake local drainage and sewage maintenance functions.

METROPOLITAN AREAS
Following the 1986 reorganisation prompted by the **Local Government Act 1985** single-tier local government was introduced to the metropolitan areas. **London Boroughs** have been responsible for the following since 1964:–Personal Social Services, Environmental Health, Licensing, Libraries and Swimming Baths, Trading Standards, Registration of Births, Marriages and Deaths, Land Charges, Allotments, Cemeteries and Crematoria, Street Cleansing, Local Plans and Development Control, Markets, Local Roads, Local Traffic and Parking Schemes, Local Drains and Watercourses, Refuse Collection, Control of Building Construction (outer London), Civil Defence, Historic Buildings and support of the Arts.

In 1980 housing was also transferred from the Greater London Council to the boroughs. Education in inner London is the responsibility of the Inner London Education Authority.

METROPOLITAN DISTRICTS
With effect from 1st April 1974 metropolitan districts have been responsible for the following:
Education, Social Services, Libraries, Planning, Building Regulations, Housing, Environmental Health, Roads, Refuse Collection, Playing Fields and Swimming Baths, Car Parks, Museums and Art Galleries, Cemeteries and Crematoria, Markets and Fairs, Parks and Open Spaces.

IMPACT OF THE 1986 METROPOLITAN REORGANISATION
Following the abolition of the GLC and metropolitan counties, the **Local Government Act 1986** created seven Residuary Bodies to oversee the dismantling of the upper tier. Membership of these bodies is in the gift of the Secretary of State for the Environment. Their functions are as follows:
* repayment of loans incurred by the GLC and MCCs
* Redundancy payments to former employees and the administration of the GLC/MCC superannuation schemes.
*Disposal of GLC/MCC assets.

The Residuary Bodies are precepting authorities and must wind up their activities by April 1st 1991.

After abolition the following additional services were transferred to the London boroughs and metropolitan districts: Planning, National Parks, Highways and Traffic, Waste Regulation and Disposal, Land Drainage and

Flood Prevention (MCC areas only), Magistrates Courts, Coroners and Local Valuation Panels.

Aside from being the only single-tier administrative units in British local government, the seven metropolitan areas share the disadvantage of only receiving the product of a twopenny rate from their Section 137 Miscellaneous Provision Act powers unlike the 4p available in some areas. These powers, confirmed by successive Local Government Finance Acts, allow local authorities to raise the product of a twopenny rate for areas of expenditure not covered by existing legislation. Grants to voluntary groups are often culled from this source. In shire areas both the district and county tiers of Government have the power of a twopenny rate. However, following reorganisation in 1986, metropolitan districts did not receive the transferred power to levy for the abolished county tier.

Joint Committees were established to oversee Strategic Planning, Police (MCC areas only), Fire and Civil Defence, Passenger Transport and Airports.

RELATIONSHIP WITH CENTRAL GOVERNMENT

The main focus for consultation with central Government lies with the local authority associations. There are three national bodies in England namely the Association of County Councils, the Association of District Councils (and its Welsh Committee with offices in Cardiff), and the Association of Metropolitan Authorities. In Scotland, the Convention of Scottish Local Authorities negotiates with the Scottish Office on behalf of Regions and district councils.

London has its own separate representative bodies, namely the London Boroughs Association and the Association of London Authorities, both of whom are accorded consultative status by the Department of the Environment. Nevertheless, some boroughs also hold membership of the LBA, ALA and the AMA.

These Associations safeguard the interests of their constituent members. They scrutinise proposed legislation. They make representations to the departments of central Government on matters which affect the councils they represent. In all this the Associations are assisted by their permanent secretariats in London (and Edinburgh, in Scotland). When a particular council wishes to put forward views on a matter of national importance, or to press for changes in the law, it will usually do so by sending its views forward to its Association in the first place.

The political groupings on the Associations reflect the membership, but despite this the Associations often agree a bipartisan view on issues that affect local government.

The Department of the Environment is the principal Government department but various consultative councils and working parties deal with other Government ministries such as the DHSS.

A full breakdown of the structure of consultation is provided in the diagram shown on the next page.

OTHER NATIONAL BODIES

The **Local Authorities Conditions of Service Advisory Board** or LACSAB is the focal point for most of the central activities of local authorities in connection with the settlement of wages, salaries and conditions of service. These are negotiated nationally through a network of National Joint Councils and Committees, on which sit representatives of both employers and trade unions. The national arrangements are supported by Provincial Councils. Local authorities in each provincial area nominate members to the employers side of the various panels dealing with manual workers, roadmen, salaried staff and so on. LACSAB is responsible with the Department of the Environment and the Secretary of State for Scotland for the Joint Manpower Watch which is compiled quarterly, based on staff returns from local authorities. The National Joint

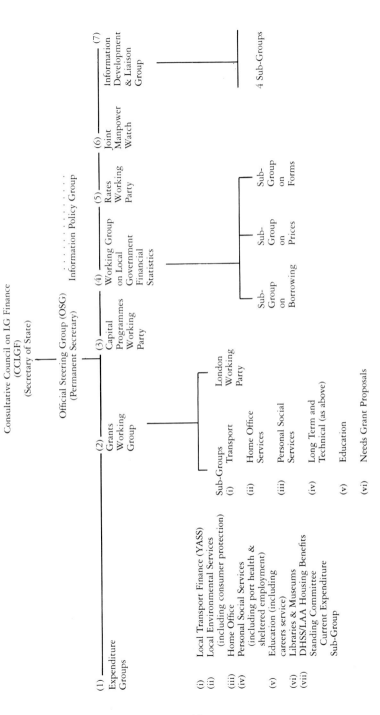

Council for Local Authorities Service (Scottish Council) is located in Edinburgh. The **Local Government Training Board** has wide responsibilities for ensuring the adequate training of the staffs of local authorities. It analyses national training needs and sponsors and supports training courses. The Training Board is also responsible for reviewing existing training methods and preparing training material. The Board assists the work of training officers of authorities. It also works closely with the Provincial Council training officers and can assist those authorities who have no training officer of their own, to organise day-release, in-service training courses and the like.

LAMSAC provides central expertise on organisation and methods, on work study and computer developments. Besides its publications, research activities and conferences, LAMSAC also provides general advisory services to any individual local aauthority which seeks detailed advice on modern computer management methods. LAMSAC also has an office in Edinburgh which provides its services to Scottish local authorities.

The **Local Government Boundary Commissions** have the task of keeping under review the areas of local authorities. Their powers are very wide and include the constitution of a new authority, the abolition of an existing one, the conversion of a metropolitan into a non-metropolitan district or vice versa. The Commission also have a duty to keep under review the electoral arrangements in counties and districts. There are separate Commissions for England, Wales and Scotland.

THE MANAGEMENT OF LOCAL GOVERNMENT

Management in local government has a history of being dominated by trends and fashion. The classic bureaucratic model based on a vertical decision ladder formed the basis for management in local government from the mid 1880s to the late 1960s.

However, following the **Maud Report** in 1967, and more fundamentally the **Bains Report** in 1974, a new type of thinking imported from the American private sector hit local government. 'Corporate management' as it became known had a significant impact on the local government scene for the best part of a decade. The idea was to end departmentalism with directors building their own empires and refusing to view the council as a homogenous organisation, content instead to further the expansion of their own department.

The Bains report also introduced the concept of the chief executive. Prior to this the Clerk to the Council, although head of the officer corps was – by training – a lawyer. His role was adviser to members on all legal and administrative matters. But management – in its fullest sense – of the organisation was not felt to be within his remit. Instead, directors managed their own departments, although they in turn were responsible to the Clerk.

Bains argued for the creation of a single post of chief executive who would lead his team of officers and he was to be responsible for 'considering the council's general problems and for co-ordinating action to solve them.' The Committee felt that the use of management teams and resource committees would enable chief officers to 'reflect the close relationship between the various services and correspond to the reduction in the number of committees'.

Unfortunately this latter recommendation fostered a suspicion among elected members that corporate management was a means of reducing the control of the elected councillor. The emergence of the 'corporate plan' – a rigid strategy document setting targets for specified goals, also paved the way for the demise of corporatism in local government. Aside from other matters, corporate planning implies a degree of certainty about future financial income, and as changes in block grant diminished the ability to forecast, the system was soon discredited.

The current penchant for accountable local government has led to the spread of decentralisation – the very antithesis of corporate management. Neighbourhood offices and even – in some cases – neighbourhood chief executives, have been introduced in some authorities. One inevitable impact of this movement which directly affects elected members is the implied increase in workload. Also, the emergence of the neighbourhood office will enable the councillor to illustrate very dramatically his effectiveness to his electorate. Decentralisation places the town hall in the community and the local councillor under the microscope. It is a very bold experiment!

THE DECISION-MAKING SYSTEM

Detailed administrative decisions can be made at three levels of a local authority. First, the full council may decide upon a course of action. Second, a committee or sub-committee may decide, or third, in special circumstances and under delegated powers, an officer may act on behalf of the authority.

The guidelines for the running and procedure of committee meetings are to be found in the Standing Orders supplied to each elected member. Standing Orders vary from authority to authority and it is vital that every new member makes the effort to wade through the inevitable legal jargon to fully understand his council's system.

There are few statutory committees. The **Local Government Act 1972** listed three committees which relevant councils must convene. These are an education, police and a social services committee.

Inevitably there are likely to be many more committees such as policy and finance but the membership of the statutory committees is prescribed in the legislation and you cannot co-opt members onto these committees. However, for all other committees, outside individuals may be co-opted on the proviso that two-thirds of the committee consist of members of the council. This numerical limitation does not apply to sub-committees.

With the exception of the statutory committees, the full council may delegate powers to committees or sub-committees to make decisions on behalf of the council, other than the power to raise money.

The full council does however retain the power to make decisions within the scope of the delegated area, but it cannot rescind decisions already made in its name by the lesser committee. It can nevertheless remove members of the committee or abolish it entirely!

Meetings of the full council are presided over by the chairman of mayor. Procedure is laid down by the Standing Orders of the authority. Members of the press and public are permitted to attend these meetings.

The 1960 Public Bodies (Admission to Meetings) Act 1980 together with Section 100 of the Local Government Act 1972, latterly amended by the Local Government (Access to Information) Act 1985 placed a duty on the council to notify the press and public of the dates, times and places at which meetings of the council or its committees of sub-committees are to be held. Both the press and public are granted a right of access by the legislation. It is only in respect of items which might involve the disclosure of very closely defined exempt information that a council may resolve to exlcude the press and public whilst such items are under consideration. Within a reasonable period after each meeting has taken place the minutes of that meeting must be available for public inspection, together with a summary of the matters that have been discussed in confidential session. The reports that are considered in the public part of the council or committee meetings must list the background papers which the author has taken into account in preparing the report, so that councillors and the public may satisfy themselves that all relevant considerations have been taken into account. Members of the the public also have the right to examine background papers listed in council reports, at the offices of the local authority.

The Access to Information Act also provides extended rights to councillors in respect of the inspection of council documents which contain material relating to any business to be transacted at a council or committee or sub-committee meeting.

OFFICERS AND DEPARTMENTS

In the majority of cases the administration of a council's business is carried out by the departments of the local authority which are each headed by a chief officer. In all but a handful of authorities the officer structure is led by a chief executive.

Under the direction of the council, the chief executive provides leadership for the other chief officers, who form a management team under his guidance. The chief executive with the management team both provide advice to the council and committees on their policies, and secures the effective implementation of the council's programme. The management team should be used to assist councillors to see clearly what policy options are available to them and what will be the likely consequences of those options.

The management team is not there to usurp the functions of the councillors: it is there to help them carry out their role more effectively. The chief officer is usually a professional in the subject of his department. However, there is currently a move away from this trend and there have been examples of directors of environmental health running social services departments. Although corporate management has been largely discredited many of the values of management enshrined in the concept have been salvaged. The departments of the authority run the various services of the council. They prepare reports and submit proposals. As a member of a committee, or even a committee chairman, an elected member will become aware of the tendency for departments to see themselves in isolation from the rest of the council. It is in the best interests of the council and the councillors to retain a council-wide perspective to counteract this trend. The councillor begins by being interested in the community, but can end by being merely a departmental watchdog. One practical means of overcoming this problem is the use of project teams in which officers from different departments work together. Such project teams should have a clear role and method of working. Well-directed central committees and the involvement of members in overall policy reviews can also be powerful instruments in securing a non-departmental approach.

FINANCE

At the heart of every decision is the question of expenditure. It is crucial for any elected member to have at the very least an understanding of the local government finance system. There are those who deliberately attempt to shroud the subject in mystery. 'If you can understand the block grant system you deserve a medal' etc. But, the complexities that govern the make-up of grant are for the civil servants at Marsham Street. You have at your disposal a resident expert in the shape of the Director of Finance, but to make a positive contribution to the running of your council's affairs it really is worth the effort to get a grip on the subject.

There are one or two excellent summaries which go into greater depth than this handbook can hope to provide. One that is strongly recommended is produced by the Association of County Councils. It labours under the imaginative title of **Understanding Block Grant – a Guide and Glossary**. Despite its usefulness it is also very cheap and its 25 pages should be essential reading for every councillor.

The council's formal budget meeting is the culmination of a long process involving all departments and committees, but placing a particular responsibility on the policy and resources committee (or any equivalent committee concerned with financial resources) advised by the Chief Executive and Director of Finance. That process is likely to involve every councillor since the financial regulations of the authority normally require each committee to prepare estimates of its expenditure in the coming year. That process can involve the councillor in hard and difficult choices – particularly in periods where financial cutbacks are required of an authority. The councillor should be satisfied that the form on which the estimates are presented highlights the choices that are to be made.

However, the committee budgetary work is only a preliminary to the budget-making process. The council must then take account of its likely income. This is derived from charges and rents, specific grants for items such as urban programme, and Rate Support Grant.

Dealing with the latter first, an authority's RSG is arrived at in the following way:

Each council has a **Grant Related Expenditure Assessment** known colloquially either as a GRE or GREA. The GREA is the means by which the Government determines that a standard level of service is available throughout the country. Inevitably, some areas are wealthier than others due, for example, to concentrations of commercial property. The Government calculates each council's GREA taking into account up to 60 factors to provide an assessment of the level of need in each area. The idea is that GREAs ensure that block grant is equally distributed among the 300-plus councils in England and Wales.

In addition to GREAs, the Government makes one other assumption, this time about the yield of local rate income. This assumed rate levy is known as the **Grant Related Poundage**.

From a fixed base, or where need equals income, the Government derives the **Grant Related Poundage Schedule**. This schedule is an important weapon in the Government's arsenal to curtail local spending. Annually the Government sets a pre-determined threshold beyond which the schedule rises steeply. Consequently, any local authority that opts to spend above the threshold loses a commensurate amount of grant.

Before 1982, local authorities could 'top up' their income in exceptional circumstances by levying a supplementary rate. However, the **Local Government Finance Act 1982** outlawed this practice. It was at this point that 'creative accountancy' came into its own as a talking point in local government. Creative accountancy is not new, it is simply the means by which accountants maximise the income available to their local authority.

Returning to the question of block grant. Once the Government has determined the GREA and GRP of a local authority, final adjustments are made to take account of year-by-year grant changes brought about by changes in GREAs or other like factors. These adjustments are known as **multipliers**. As an example of the way in which they are used, multipliers were employed to cushion the financial affects of abolishing the GLC and metropolitan counties. When all of these factors have been taken into account the Department of the Environment can then arrive at a provisional grant estimate. These figures are usually made known in November or December of each year.

All things being equal the Director of Finance can advise members of the likely impact of their spending programme taking account of the poundage schedule, unless your authority is subject to **rate limitation**.

The Rates Act 1984 introduced rate limitation as a means of curbing excessive rate rises. Ratecapping as it is more commonly known was first used in 1985/86. The criteria for selection was as follows. Any council that had spent 6% above its expenditure target (targets were abolished in 1985) and 20% above its GREA was to be given a maximum expenditure limit. Any authority selected for ratecapping was legally bound to make a rate up to its expenditure limit. If a rate was struck beyond its limit ratepayers were not obliged to pay it. Rate limitation continues, but the criteria for selection is subject to change year-on-year. An appeals procedure is built into the Act whereby an authority may seek a redetermination of its maximum expenditure limit.

In its first year of operation some of the 18 councils selected staged a protest by delaying the setting of a rate. This led to councillors on two authorities facing surcharge actions – Lambeth and Liverpool. It also led to the **Local Government Act 1986** which laid a statutory duty upon all local authorities to set a rate by April 1st of each financial year.

But rate support grant is not the only source of income to a local authority. Rates are the second source. Rates are a tax on the occupation of property levied according to the assessed rental value. This tax is levied on industrial and commercial properties. Agricultural land is not rated. In Scotland, industrial property is derated to the extent of 50%. Non-domestic property (including shops, factories etc) pay about 55% of the national rate bill. The percentage will vary from one area to another depending on the size of the commercial and industrial sector.

The third element of income comes from rents, fees and charges. These are borne directly by the user of the service. They should be kept regularly under review. The level of fees and charges should be as much a part of the budgetary process as the rate to be set.

SCOTLAND

In Scotland, the Secretary of State gives local authorities 'guidelines' in respect of their net relevant expenditure and has power to recover from them generally, according to the grant distribution formula, the amount by which the guidelines in total are exceeded by the estimated expenditure of all local authorities, to the extent to which he considers it to be excessive and unreasonable. Ratecapping also exists north of the border. However, pending legislation intends to introduce a community charge in place of domestic rates. The proposal is to collect business rates centrally and make all local authority residents subject to a community charge set by the Secretary of State and individual local authorities.

THE AUDIT FUNCTION

In addition to abolishing supplementary rates, the **Local Government Finance Act 1982** established the Audit Commission, which in its few short years of existence has had a profound impact upon local government.

An independent body, the Commission – which absorbed the district audit service – has a Chairman who is appointed by the Secretary of State and a board made up of 17 representatives drawn from the local authority associations, industry, trade unions and the accounting profession. Its objectives are to appoint auditors to local authorities and to help authorities to bring about improvements in efficiency, directly through the auditing process and through the 'value for money' studies which the Commission carries out.

Although the Commission has fostered an image of seeking efficiency and value for money in local government, it has also made full use of its Section 27 powers. This was the section of the 1982 Act which empowered the Commission to investigate and report on the impact of statutory provisions. To date the Commission has aroused controversy by questioning – among other things – the basis of the Rate Support Grant system and the annuality of the system for controlling capital spending.

The Commission is also responsible for the appointment of auditors from the private sector to local government after consultation with the authority concenred. currently, private firms are only used in a small number of cases with the bulk of the audit work going to district audit staff. In pursuit of this function the Commission sets a scale of audit fees on an annual basis.

It is a statutory requirement that the accounts of local authorities be subject to an external audit annually. The time and place of the audit must be advertised in the local press. The accounts have to be placed on deposit, with supporting vouchers, and can be inspected by any interested person. Any local government elector has the right to object to any item in the accounts to the district auditor. If the complainant is not satisfied with the auditor's decision, he has recourse to the High Court.

The auditor has wide-ranging powers of access to documents and information, and the report which must be made to the council may include any matter arising which the auditor feels is of concern to the public interest. The report must be circulated and the Press cannot be excluded during discussion of it.

In light of recent cases, this is an appropriate moment to mention **surcharge**. Surcharge actions are, in normal circumstances, brought by the district auditor. Surcharge normally arises when an item of account is unlawful, ie the authority has exceeded its legal powers.

However, before the Clay Cross, Lambeth and Liverpool cases, surcharge was more closely associated with cases of corruption. As an elected member councillors have to be doubly vigilant in their dealings with outside parties, particularly those seeking planning permission from the council or contracts from the council to undertake works or services.

It is worth bearing in mind that the offering, giving, soliciting or acceptance of any inducement or reward which does, or is intended to, influence the decision of the council or one of its committees in respect of such an item, is a criminal offence which is punishable by imprisonment.

At this stage, any member interested in this area, should turn to the chapter headed **Members and the Law** which discusses the declaration of interest. Members are under a duty to declare any pecuniary interests that they have in any matter which is before a council committee and then leave the meeting without taking part in the discussion or voting. A more grey area is that of the non-pecuniary interest. Guidance on surcharge in general and declaration of interest, pecuniary and otherwise, should always be sought from the council solicitor.

Where the auditor believes that an item is unlawful he may apply to the High Court. The court can require those responsible for the illegal expenditure to make repayment in whole or part. If the expenditure exceeds £2,000 the court can also order disqualification from membership of a local authority for a specified period.

More severe are the penalties for what is known as a section 20 offence. Persons responsible for a failure to bring a relevant sum into account or for loss caused by wilful misconduct are liable to repay the amount involved regardless of the circumstances. In this context wilful misconduct has been defined as 'deliberately doing something which is wrong, knowing it to be wrong or with reckless indifference as to whether it is wrong or not'. If they are elected members and the amount again exceeds £2,000, they are automatically disqualified from membership of a local authority for five years. Those named in a certificate may appeal against it to the courts.

If a councillor – or for that matter an officer – can show that he acted reasonably or in the belief that the expenditure was authorised by law, the courts are empowered to quash the certificate.

In Scotland, it is the function of the Accounts Commission to secure the audit of accounts using its own staff or the services of private accountants. Each local authority must make an abstract of its accounts available for public inspection and any person may object to the auditor about any part of the accounts. The auditor reports to the **Controller of Audit**, the principal officer of the Commission, who may in turn bring any matter arising from the accounts to the attention of the local authority and/or the public. The Accounts Commission predates the Audit Commission, but like its southern counterpart, is independent of both central and local government. Members of the Commission are appointed by the Secretary of State for Scotland and the members of the Commission appoint the Controller.

Unlike England, however, if a discrepancy is found in the accounts of a local authority, a special report is published and a further report is made to the Secretary of State. It is then up to the Minister to decide if surcharge action should follow.

THE OMBUDSMAN

In 1974 a foreign import was introduced to the local government scene, from Scandinavia. Called the Commission for Local Administration but more commonly known as the Ombudsman, the **Local Government Act** 1974 (and for Scotland, the **Local Government (Scotland Act) 1975** introduced a new appeals procedure for members of the public in cases of alleged maladministration.

Maladministration is not defined by the legislation but includes such factors as neglect, bias, unfairness, incompetence and excessive delay.

The Ombudsman is really an appeal of last resort since the Commissioners cannot consider a complaint where alternative means of redress exist, and complaints should – in theory – be made via a councillor. In fact there is an increasing number of complaints being made direct to the Ombudsman, who is obliged to contact the local authority – usually the mayor or chief executive – when this occurs.

Where the Ombudsman decides to investigate a complaint, he or she must afford the authority concerned – and any named parties – an opportunity to comment. Ombudsmen have the power to require that relevant information be supplied to them and they have the same powers as the High Court in respect of the attendance and examination of witnesses.

A Commissioner is **excluded** from considering complaints in the following areas:
* matters affecting all or most of the inhabitants
* matters concerning markets, docks and harbours, entertainments and passenger transport undertakings
* management or discipline in schools
* personnel matters
* normally any matter in which the complainant has a right of appeal to any court, tribunal or Minister of the Crown.

On completion of his investigation, which must be conducted in private, the Ombudsman is obliged to report his findings to the council concerned. The council is bound to consider the report. However, if no action is subsequently taken, the Ombudsman can issue a second report and repeat the procedure. Nevertheless, if the authority decides to ignore his report, the matter ends there. The Commissioner is a mediator of conscience. He has no powers of penalty or any other means of enforcement.

Councillors should be prepared to advise members of the public as to their rights to refer matters to the Ombudsman.

The addresses for the Commissioners are:

ENGLAND   21 Queen Anne's Gate, London SW1H 9BU

WALES   Derwen House, Court Road, Bridgend CF31 1BN

SCOTLAND   5 Shandwick Place, Edinburgh EH2 4RG

THE ELECTED MEMBER

TENURE

County councillors are elected for a period of four years to represent electoral divisions; all retire together. District councillors represent wards; in metropolitan districts, one-third retire in each year. In shire districts, councillors can either follow the metropolitan example or retire as a whole council every fourth year. In London, terms of office are for three years: councillors retire together.

A council cannot expel one of its members, but a member's seat becomes vacant if he absents himself from meetings for six consecutive months without leave.

PARTY POLITICS AND LOCAL GOVERNMENT

Mention has already been made of the role of political parties in the national local authority associations, but whereas 25 years ago politics and local government were insignificant, today they are inseparable.

It is true that in certain councils, the independent councillor outnumbers the political councillor, but this is now the exception rather than the rule.

In some councils there are conventions, written or unwritten, which govern the relations between rival parties. These conventions govern such things as the allocation of seats on committees; the holding of chairmanships and vice-chairmanships; and the representation of minority parties at official functions or at local government conferences.

Increasingly it is the practice for the party groups to meet before important meetings of the authority. Such meetings are almost always held before the council meeting itself, but in many authorities a group meeting precedes all important committees. At these pre-meetings the agenda is discussed and lines of action agreed.

It is usual, where there is a political majority, for the ruling party to take all of the committee chairmanships. It may have a central policy-making committee which is composed only of its own members. The minority party may to a degree be forced into the role of opposition, very much as in Parliament. In councils with a developed political system of this sort, the chief executive and chief officers will tend to develop a special relationship with the majority party leadership. This does not mean that they will have abandoned their traditionally non-political stance, any more than civil servants do by the convention that they serve only the Government of the day.

Where the new councillor is a member of a minority party in such a politically run council, he must expect some limits to the advice and help which officials may feel able to give him. Whilst this will be unlimited as to matters of factual information and procedural guidance, it will be circumscribed in the area of policy formulation and advice. In a well-developed political system, there tends to be a closer identification of the administration with the party in power for the time being. This is a fact of life which must be accepted.

HUNG COUNCILS

In recent years the number of authorities without a clear political majority has increased dramatically.

Depending on how long the authority has been hung, systems to overcome the implied confusion will have been developed. This often includes amended – if not completely revised – Standing Orders and a new code of guidance for dealing with the press.

The first 12 months of coming to terms with the lack of a political majority can be traumatic, especially during the budget round. However, many authorities have come to terms with the new system with remarkable success. Cheshire County Council is a case in point. Here a well-developed machinery for guiding officer/councillor relations plus dealings with the media has been negotiated between the political parties and the chief executive. The text of this framework has been reproduced with permission of the county council in the appendices of this handbook and is recommended reading to any councillor newly elected to an authority lacking central political control.

THE MANY ROLES OF THE COUNCILLOR

A councillor has been elected not only to represent his area on the council but also to take decisions affecting the area of the authority as a whole. He has been cast for many different roles. He will not necessarily give the same emphasis to each one. At different moments he will choose to emphasise one role rather than another. The council requires councillors to play different parts, and benefits from varying emphasis.

- A councillor has to represent his area. He cannot afford to neglect its special problems or to ignore issues that arise in it.
- A councillor has to deal with the problems and issues raised by individual constituents.
- A councillor must be concerned to ensure that the administration of the council is both fair and efficient.
- A councillor must be concerned that the resources of the authority are fully utilised and that the priorities for competing resources are fairly assessed.
- A councillor must help to determine the policies to be pursued by the council, not only for activities in which he has a special interest, but those which concern the council as a whole.

The problem for a councillor and for a council is to achieve a balance between those different roles. None can ever be completely neglected. Even the most junior member of the council will be called upon to vote upon major issues and policy. Even the most senior member of the council will have to consider the problems of an individual constituent.

An effective council depends upon balance between the roles. It is right that the special problems of an area be raised in a council, but right too that the council is able to consider those problems against the general policies of the council. Equally it is perfectly acceptable for a councillor to interest himself in special areas of activity, so long as he weighs those particular interests against other interests. Nevertheless, all general policies should be tested and modified to meet changing problems, and these may well be highlighted by a councillor dealing with individual grievances.

A councillor who is captured by one role, or a council that over-emphasises one role, has lost the balance that makes its contribution effective.

As the council contains many roles, so too it provides many settings. Each setting has its own conventions and atmosphere. The council and the committee have already been described as part of the council machinery. But there are other settings which are important for the councillor. The party group, the party meeting, the councillor's surgery are all important settings for the councillor's work as are meetings with officers to discuss problems, or informal policy groups set up by committees to explore policy issues. Council work should never be regarded as restricted to the formal business of council and committees.

THE COMMITTEE MEETING

A newly elected councillor has a great deal to learn in a short space of time. Obviously there are dangers in the newly elected member intervening in issues when he knows little of the background, but there are means of getting around this.

Where the councillor does not feel he has sufficient information in the papers supplied, he should ask the officer who is presenting the report for the required information – preferably before the meeting. He should ask for background papers on the matter under discussion. This will both ensure that he obtains the information and will help the officer to understand the problems of the councillor.

Nevertheless, there will be times when the questioning approach of the newcomer can bring a challenge to practices which those long-established in council affairs take for granted.

The main breaking-in point for the new councillor will be through the committee or committees to which he is appointed. The custom in appointing to committees varies. Increasingly it is dealt with through the party machine. The newly elected councillor is quite likely to find that, however the selection is made, he is not on the committee of his first choice. Pressure for places on certain committees tends to result in the newly elected councillor being placed on the less popular committees.

This may well mean that the councillor is on a committee dealing with activities and issues with which he is relatively unfamiliar or in which he has relatively less interest and less, in his view, to offer. He may well find that the business of the committee is conducted as if all those who attend are familiar with everything that has gone before. There will be reference to Acts or Regulations with which the new councillor is unfamiliar. There will be references to previous decisions of the committee or previous policy decisions of the council. Again, the elected member should turn to the director of the relevant department for information and, if necessary, briefings on the department and its workings.

HINTS ON COMMITTEE WORK

The councillor will receive masses of papers. He will receive agendas for committees and council – each with supporting reports. He will receive additional material. He will receive correspondence. He faces major problems in assimilating this material.

The councillor is always short of time. He will sometimes, for example, find it impossible to have studied carefully all the papers for a committee meeting. He may have to select. There is an art in sifting the chaff from the wheat in committee papers which comes with practice. But a councillor should not accept so much committee work that he cannot find time to read the papers sent to him.

The councillor should select certain items on an agenda for examination in depth. He can select them by their intrinsic importance, by the fact that he has special knowledge or interest in them, or by their impact on his electorate. It is useful to have these three approaches since the last two provide a test for the apparently unimportant item.

He can apply some rough tests, even to a topic on which he has no expert knowledge:

– Why is this proposal being brought forward?
– What will it achieve?
– What alternatives have been considered?
– What resources are to be used?
– What assumptions have been made?
– How valid are the assumptions made?
– What recommendations are made for review of the impact of this proposal if agreed?

Answers to these elementary questions will help the councillor to evaluate the report.

Where a councillor has particular knowledge relating to a proposal made, because of its impact on his electoral district, it is important to use that knowledge as a test bed – even if the proposal conforms with accepted policy. This does not mean that a councillor should claim special treatment for his electoral district. It does, however, enable him to consider the impact of policy on a particular case or situation. This will enable him to judge whether the policy itself is soundly based or whether it requires review. It is against the councillor's particular knowledge that policies can best be tested.

Many authorities are moving towards a position in which each committee has the opportunity to consider at least once a year the broad direction of its policies. This could be done in a day-long meeting or even a week-end seminar to examine performance in the activities for which it is responsible. The agenda could centre on a major policy review examining past achievements and failures, new problems, and unresolved issues and looking ahead over the coming years. It could help to establish priorities for the committee and guide the problem of resource allocation. Reviews of performance, policies and problems are likely to be especially important and valuable in periods of financial restraint.

There is one remaining problem about committee work. The councillor will face a problem in filing. At an early stage he must decide how many papers he wants to keep and how they should be filed. Some authorities provide files for members to keep papers in, and maintain a reference library in which the councillor can get ready access to copies of all minutes and other proceedings of the authority – much of it often on computer. This enables the member to concentrate on filing only those papers dealing with issues of some degree of permanent importance. Some authorities also provide new members with background papers and information – on the whole few grumble at having insufficient reading material!

ELECTORS PROBLEMS

Some councillors hold surgeries at which electors can raise problems. Other councillors are contacted directly by their electors – by phone, by letter or at their home. The councillor has a responsibility to listen to his electors and to deal with the issues they raise. He has also a responsibility to explain in his area the policies and programmes of the authority. There will be occasions when the councillor cannot support the elector, because the issue raised by the elector is a direct result of policy known to and supported by the councillor; but many of the issues raised will be the result of policies in which the councillor has not been directly involved, or the result of administrative action. In such cases the councillor will wish to pursue the points raised. It is important to do so, even in those instances where the councillor anticipates the likely reply.

The councillor should raise the elector's query with the appropriate department or departments. He may do so by letter, by telephone or in person. In a large authority with many staff, it is sensible to raise the issue shortly by letter or to make an appointment, so that the department concerned can ascertain the facts and have their file of papers available at any discussion which may be arranged.

The councillor should critically appraise any reply given. Normally that reply will be acceptable and in accordance with established policy. But it is important that the councillor identifies instances where the results of established policy appear to have led to unfairness or hardship.

He should notify his elector of the reply and listen to any comments he may have. In the final resort he has to determine in each case how far a matter is to be pursued. It will be rare that he will want to put down a question or notice of motion for a meeting of the council so that the elector's problems can be answered or debated in public. Nevertheless, in the last resort, these avenues are open to the diligent councillor and he should not be afraid to use them when he has enough experience. The important issue is that the councillor is fair to the elector, to himself and to the authority.

THE PRESS

There is a lot of truth in the adage that you get the press coverage you deserve. More than ever before, the work of the local authority is in the public eye, and an elected member should expect to be questioned by reporters from the newspapers, radio and television.

If a councillor makes a speech at a meeting open to the press its contents may well be reported in local or national newspapers. You should remember that many local paper reporters regularly supply stories to the nationals. Clearly then, one obvious way a councillor can air his views to a wider audience than a council committee is by peppering his speech with controversial remarks. However, before any elected member embarks upon this course, he should give heed to the laws of **defamation**.

DEFAMATION

A defamatory statement is one that directs scorn, ridicule or contempt at an individual or body of individuals which may injure the victim's reputation in the eyes of the world. Written defamatory matter is called libel and spoken defamatory matter is called slander.

Defamation actions are expensive and require the sanction of a judge in chambers before they can go ahead. It is a defence that the statement was true, or was fair comment on a matter of public interest, or was made on a privileged occasion.

Privilege – or exemption – from defamatory action is afforded to judicial proceedings, proceedings in Parliament and to communications between High Officers of State.

Qualified privilege can be extended to accurate newspaper reports or radio/television broadcasts of parliamentary proceedings and public meetings. This clause includes council meetings. The defence of privilege can only be used where there is proof of absence of malice. In these circumstances malice is defined as a desire to hurt or injure the person spoken of. Furthermore, if the defamer makes his remarks without having bothered to check or care whether they were true or not, the person making the statement is treated as having known it was false in the first place.

If an individual is unintentionally defamed, the publisher may make amends by printing an apology at the earliest opportunity.

DEALING WITH REPORTERS

However, a new councillor need not go in fear and dread of defamation. So long as he avoids malicious personal attacks, he should view the press as a useful tool.

Electors like to know that their councillor is fighting their corner and local papers — particularly — are an ideal vehicle for communicating with voters. There are, however, one or two things that should be kept in mind. Newspapers are not interested in good news unless it is exceptionally good news. If you have succeeded in getting a zebra crossing designated in an area of high road casualties, then clearly that is of interest to the press. However, if you have also succeeded in getting a vandalised wall painted, this is unlikely to set the pulses racing on the local newsdesks.

If a councillor is contacted for information and he is in any doubt about the matter, it is better to arrange to call back the newspaper in question. This will allow the councillor time to make inquiries and decide what can and should be said. There is always a danger in an unguarded off-the-cuff comment which may quite properly be used by the media, but which does not fully and adequately represent the councillor's view.

Similarly, it is also advisable to get to know the journal or newspaper you are dealing with. What is its style? Is it inclined to blow things out of proportion? Is the reporter on the other end of the telephone line a responsible journalist who is able to ensure that what he writes is accurately printed? It is often the case that a reporter's story is radically changed by the sub-editors, who are short of a hard-hitting piece. There are no hard and fast rules to avoid getting 'burned'. It is almost inevitable that at some stage in your career in public life that you will be misquoted and taken out of context.

However, you should accept this — so far as possible — and consider the free publicity that you and your party — if you belong to a political group — are getting. No news is completely bad news. Finally, this is a difficult area but one that can be rewarding. Many local authorities have press and public relations staff. A new councillor should always talk to council press staff and equally should expect reporters to always **avoid** council press staff. It is a good idea to ask for a briefing both on newspapers, journals etc that are likely to contact the council, and the reporters that are likely to phone. Forewarned is forearmed!

Before leaving this subject, mention should be made of the impact of the hung council on press and public relations. Where there is no ruling group, the chief executive, in consultation with the leaders of the respective groups, will usually draft a code for dealing with the press. This is done to avoid confusion, and to present at least a coherent image to the outside world. In the appendices are printed the regulations and code of conduct adopted by Cheshire County Council. If your authority does not have a code, it is well worth reading the Cheshire guidelines as a useful reference.

MEMBERS AND THE LAW

The councillor has certain rights and certain obligations. It is important that he understands both.

a) Paid appointment

A councillor is not permitted to accept any paid appointment from the council except in the position of chairman and vice-chairman of the council. He is also debarred from accepting any such appointment for 12 months after he ceases to be a member.

b) Disclosure of interest by council members

A member who has a direct or indirect financial interest in a matter arising before the council or any of its committees must disclose that interest as soon as practicable, and he is disqualified from speaking or voting on that matter save where his interest is so remote or insignificant that it cannot reasonably be regarded as likely to influence him. Failure to comply with these requirements is a criminal offence, and if a disqualified member takes part in any proceedings analogous to that of a judicial tribunal (eg where the council is exercising licensing functions), the decision can be quashed by the courts. A member of a local authority is required to declare all of his pecuniary interests.

The duty to disclose lies firmly on the member. It is no part of the duty of the council's legal officers to remind a member that he may have an interest to disclose. Nevertheless it is usual for the council's legal advisers to help a member with advice, as it is sometimes difficult to interpret the legal provisions contained in Sections 94–98 of the **Local Government Act 1972**. As far as Scotland is concerned, it is not the practice for the council's legal advisers to tender advice to members individually on questions of interest. The relevant legal provisions are contained in Sections 38–42 of the **Local Government (Scotland) Act 1973**.

A simple and usual case of disclosure arises when a councillor owns a business which has tendered for a council contract. The interest is 'direct' if the councillor owns the business. It is 'indirect' if he is a member of a company or other body or is a partner in a firm or is employed by a person with whom the contract is proposed to be made. Whereas a 'contract' is easily understood, it is more debatable what is a pecuniary interest in an 'other matter'. It has been held, for example, that the rule would apply to a policy debate as to whether a council should build by direct labour when one of the councillor's present was a building contractor.

However, the respective Acts provide that membership of a company or other body or a partnership with some other person shall not of itself create an obligation to disclose, if the interest is so remote or so insignificant that it cannot reasonably be regarded as likely to influence the member.

In the case of membership of or employment by companies, bodies or persons contracting with the council, eg directors of companies, the member may give a general notice to the 'proper officer' of the council. Such a general notice can be made when he or his spouse is (a) a member or in the employment of a specified company or other body; or (b) is a tenant of any premises owned by the council. Such a notice remains a sufficient disclosure of his interest in any of those matters until it is withdrawn. General notices of this kind will be recorded in a book kept by the proper officer which must be available for inspection by any other member of the council. The proper officer will usually be the Secretary or Director of Administration.

The Act lists a number of situations where the duty to disclose does not arise. These include:

(a)   the receipt by a member (or the likelihood of his receiving) any allowance or other payment relating to his membership of the council;

(b)   membership of or employment under any public body, eg a nationalised industry, governing body of a school or college or the National Trust;

(c)   membership of a company or other body if the councillor has no beneficial interest in any securities of that company or other body;

(d)   an interest merely by virtue of his being a ratepayer or inhabitant in the area of the authority or as an ordinary consumer of water;

(e)   an interest in any matter relating to the terms in which the right to participate in any service (including the supply of goods) is offered to the public, eg the repayment terms under which home helps would be provided to the public.

There is a special exemption for people who own shares not exceeding £1000 nominal value (or 1/100 of issued share capital if that is less) in companies with whom the council has dealings. The interest must be disclosed, but discussion and voting is permitted.

In the rare event of the number of members who would have to disclose a pecuniary interest and withdraw from a meeting being so great as to impede the transaction of council or committee business, the Secretary of State may, on request, remove the disability of all the members for a specified or unlimited period.

When complaints about the failure of a councillor to declare a non-pecuniary interest have been found by the local Ombudsman to be justified the critical findings have usually arisen:

a) When a councillor has had a direct personal link with the matter being considered, for example through living close to the site of a planning application, or being connected socially with an applicant; and

b) has actively participated in the events complained or, for example spoken on the next door neighbour's application at a committee meeting without having declared an interest.

The National code of Conduct issued in 1975 points out the 'kinship, friendhip and membership of an association, society or trade union trusteeship and many other kinds or relationship can sometimes influence your judgment and give the impression that you might be acting ror personal motives'. the Ombudsman pays particular attention to the final part of that quotation and expects a councillor to ask himself what would a reasonably-minded impartial observer think. The Ombudsman may find maladministation is his judgment of what a 'reasonably-minded external observer' would think was that the circumstances were such that the councillor would not have been able to participate in a decision on a particular topic without being influenced by perhaps the proximity of his house to the development porposed or his close friendship with the applicant.

In these circumstances the failure by the individual member to declare such an interest and to continue to participate in the debate and the vote may well result in a finding of maladministration against the council itself, even though his fellow-councillors may have had no idea of the existence of the interest in question.

The great difficulty here, and for those legal officers who will always seek to assist them with advice, is defining interpretations for general application. It is not possible to say that beyond a given distance from a particular property you do not have an interest, nor apart from a family relationship, is it possible to define precisely what level of friendship brings into play a non-pecuniary interest. Each case has to be considered on its merits on the basis of the view of this hypothetical 'reasonable external observer'.

ALLOWANCES FOR MEMBERS

The Treasurer of the council will provide new councillors with the necessary forms of claim for the various allowances to which members are entitled. It is also usual to provide explanatory notes as to what may be claimed and when. Each authority has its own procedure for making claims and for dealing with such matters as the payment of income tax on the attendance allowance. Each council will also have rules as to whether travelling time is to be counted, and whether half-a-day allowance is to be specified.

The last piece of relevant legislation dealing with allowances for members was the **Local Government Planning and Land Act 1980** which, among other things, introduced a special responsibility allowance and made group meetings an approved duty.

The maximum rates of allowance are prescribed by law. Within that maximum each council will determine how much will be paid. In the case of attendance at outside bodies, in general the allowance will be payable by the council.

However, in the case of attendance at meetings of health authorities, water authorities and local valuation panels, any allowances payable should be claimed from them and not the local authority.

The notes which follow are intended to explain the arrangements for allowances as they are incorporated in the **Local Government Act 1972**. The Department of the Environment, in Circular 16/74, said that 'local authorities should bear in mind that the attendance allowance includes an element for miscellaneous expenditure on postage, telephones etc'. Some authorities nevertheless provide for the payment of telephone rentals and have made arrangements for secretarial help to be provided for members.

A councillor is, for every approved duty, entitled to claim:
– attendance allowance
– subsistence allowance (the 1980 Act abolished the three-mile limit)

Approved duty is defined in the Act to include attendance at council meetings and meetings of committees or sub-committees of the council. Approved duty includes the doing of any other thing approved by the council for the purpose of, or in connection with, the discharge of the functions of the council or of any of its committees or sub-committees. There is, in other words (a) a statutory entitlement in the case of the council and other meetings; and (b) a discretion to the authority to enlarge the entitlement to cover the performance of other duties by councillors.

Members (including co-opted members) will be entitled to allowances for attending conferences inside or outside the UK. To qualify, the conference must not be convened by any body in the course of trade or business. They must be to discuss matters relating to the interests of the area or its inhabitants.

The allowances for councillors are:

Conference in the UK: Attendance allowance, travel and subsistence allowance not exceeding the prescribed maximum.

Conferences outside the UK: Attendance allowance, reasonable travel and subsistence.

Members may make official or courtesy visits inside or outside the UK. The councillor will, inside the UK, get the prescribed rate of travel and subsistence and, outside the UK, reasonable travel and other expenses. It is unlikely that an attendance allowance will be paid unless the visit can be brought within the 'approved duty' category.

The council must keep a record of allowances paid to councillors and the record is open to inspection by any local government elector.

A councillor may choose by written notice to be paid a financial loss allowance instead of his attendance allowance. He would be advised to consult the officers about the implications of this choice.

In Scotland, the Director of Finance deals with claims for allowances, the arrangements for which are contained in the **Local Government (Scotland) Act 1973** and regulations made thereunder.

APPENDICES

CHESHIRE COUNTY COUNCIL – STANDING ORDERS

Conventions on relations between the political parties represented on the council.

1. Introduction

1.1 The formal business of the Council is regulated by Standing Orders and other chapters of the 'Red Book'. Other important aspects of business are less easily regulated by formal rules drafted in legal or semi-legal language. These are set out for the guidance of members of the Council and chief officers in this statement of conventions.

1.2 The conventions are to be read alongside and as subordinate to the Standing Orders and other Red Book provisions.

2. Definitions

2.1 For purposes of this statement a 'Committee' refers also to a sub-committee.

2.2 'Committee Chairmen and Vice-Chairmen' are the members appointed to those offices by the Council.

2.3 'Party Spokesmen' are any members nominated by a party group not holding the chair or vice chair of a committee to be its spokesman on that committee.

3. Titles

3.1 The Chairman of the Policy and Resources Committee will be known as the Leader of the Council and the vice-chairman of that committee as the Deputy Leader of the Council.

3.2 The leader of the largest party group not holding committee chairs will be known as the Leader of the Opposition.

4. Entitlement to information

4.1 Any member of the Council may ask the appropriate chief officer for written factual information about a department or service. Such requests will be met subject to any legal requirements and to 4.2 below. A copy of the chief officer's response will be given to the chairman and party spokesmen of the appropriate committee, unless the member's letter is marked 'Personal' or the information provided is of routine or minor nature. This arrangement is additional to the provisions for briefing (see sections 5 and 6).

4.2 If a chief officer considers that information requested under 4.1 could only be provided at unreasonable cost he shall seek direction from the chairman of the committee as to whether it should be provided.

4.3 A chief officer may on his own initiative provide information as in 4.1 to a committee chairman. Such information will be supplied to the spokesmen of other parties, unless it is of a routine or minor nature.

4.4   Chief officers should keep local members informed of significant issues affecting their divisions.

5. Briefing on committee business

5.1   Formal briefings will be arranged for the chairman and vice-chairman (jointly) of committees to consider the business to be transacted at each meeting as set out on the agenda. The chairman may at his or her discretion invite spokesmen of other parties or other appropriate chairmen or vice-chairmen, to attend such briefings. Such an arrangement is without prejudice to 5.2.

5.2   Any party not holding the chair or vice-chair of a committee may request a briefing on the business to be transacted at a committee meeting. Such a request shall be made by the leader or relevant spokesman to the Chief Executive who will make the appropriate arrangements with the chief officer(s) concerned.

6. Briefing of party groups

6.1   In addition to the formal arrangements described above, all party groups may request a private and confidential briefing, including, but where appropriate going beyond, the provision of written information, on matters of policy which are or may become the subject of discussion by the Council or any committee.

6.2   Such a request shall be made by the leader or relevant spokesman of the party group concerned to the Chief Executive who will make the appropriate arrangements with the chief officer(s) concerned. A chief officer may nominate a member of his staff to provide such a briefing.

7. Filling of casual vacancies

7.1   Selection Sub-Committee is responsible for making appointments to committees under Standing Order 21 in accordance with principles agreed from time to time.

7.2   When a casual vacancy in the office of county councillor (whether consequent upon death, resignation or any other reason) arises, the appointment of members, co-opted members and other persons to committees and sub-committees, education service appointments and outside organisations to fill vacancies shall be dealt with as follows:

1. No such vacancy shall be filled until such time as the consequential by-election has taken place and the new member has presented his declaration of acceptance of office.

2. If the filling of a vacancy in representation on an outside organisation arising from the death or resignation of a member is considered to be urgent, the chairman of the Selection Sub-Committee in accordance with SO 26 may approve the filling of that vacancy.

3. Subject to the above such vacancies may be filled either:

(a) at the next ordinary meeting of the Selection Sub-Committee after the by-election has taken place and the new member has presented his or her declaration of acceptance of office;

(b) through the Chairman of the Selection Sub-Committee under SO 26 approving such proposals as may be notified to the County Secretary and Solicitor.

4. Any proposal to request the approval of the Chairman of the Selection Sub-Committee under SO 26 to the filling of any vacancy or under SO 21.4 to the mutual exchange of committee places shall be submitted to the County Secretary and Solicitor by the appropriate party group officer. Any such notice should indicate the date from which the filling/change is to take effect. No less than three clear working days notice should be allowed for the appropriate approvals to be obtained.

8. Panels established by committees

8.1 Subject to Standing Orders 21–23 a committee may establish on an ad hoc or standing basis a panel of members of the committee, excluding co-opted members, to consider an issue in more detail.

8.2 Places on panels should normally be allocated to party groups in accordance with the formulas agreed by the Selection Sub-Committee (at present 2:2:1, 3:3:1, 4:4:2 and 5:5:2) or appropriate multiples.

8.3 The Chairman of such panels shall be the Chairman of the parent committee and the membership shall where appropriate include the Vice-Chairman and party spokesman.

8.4 A party group may, on notification to the County Secretary and Solicitor, substitute another member in the place of any member who is unable to attend a panel meeting, having regard to the desirability of maintaining continuity of attendances. Any substituted member should be a member of the parent committee or sub-committee.

8.5 Panels will have delegated powers only where a specific decision must clearly be taken by the panel, eg staff appointments and disciplinary appeals or where the parent committee agrees that there are grounds of urgency. SO 31 Notices do not apply in relation to panel meetings.

8.6 For the purpose of his duty as a member, but not otherwise, a member may on application to the County Secretary and Solicitor, be supplied with a copy of the agenda and reports for any panel meeting.

8.7 The Chairman (or in the case of dispute the panel itself) may invite to panel meetings members who are not panel members or substitutes. Where a panel is to discuss a local issue, the local member or members have the right to be advised and to attend.

8.8 The minutes of all meetings of panels established by committee and sub-committee shall be submitted to the next ordinary meeting of the parent committee or sub-committee.

8.9   Subject to the above the Standing Orders of the Council shall apply to panel meetings as they apply to meetings of committees.

9. Dates of committees and panel meetings

Subject to the duty of Selection Sub-Committee to prepare the calendar of meetings of committees, proposals for the date of additional meetings and to cancel or vary the date of a meeting shall be dealt with under SO 26. Arrangements for panel meetings shall be determined by the Chairman in informal consultation with the party spokesmen.

10. Appointment of representatives

10.1   The appointment of representatives to any outside body of a permanent nature involving regular attendance will be made by the Selection Sub-Committee, confirmed when time permits by the Parliamentary and Organisation Committee. That sub-committee will also determine questions relating to approved duty.

10.2   Where an invitation to the Council to be represented at a conference or other occasion is confined to one member, the committee in question should normally be recommended to appoint the chairman or his or her nominee.

10.3   Where the invitation is to appoint more than one representative, and the occasion in the opinion of the committee so justifies, consideration should be given to appointing in addition the spokesmen of other parties or their nominees as necessary in order to achieve an appropriate political balance.

10.4   Where more than one representative is appointed to attend a conference, the chairman of the appointing committee, or in the absence of the chairman, the vice-chairman or other representatives appointed in the place of the chairman, will be regarded as the leader of the delegation. Where the delegation is entitled to cast only one vote on behalf of the County Council, that vote shall be cast by the leader in accordance with the procedure set out below. In the absence of the leader any other member of the delegation may cast the vote in accordance with the procedure.

1. Before the conference takes place any member of the delegation may request the County Secretary and Solicitor to convene a meeting of the appointed representative. Such a meeting shall be competent to settle:

(a)   the procedure to determine the policy of the Council on any issue to be raised where that is not apparent from existing Council or committee decisions;

(b)   how the vote on any issue shall be cast;

(c)   any other procedural matter germane to the conference in question.

2. In any case where the delegation may vote and the above procedure has not been followed the leader of the delegation shall first determine the wishes of each member of the delegation and shall cast the vote or abstain, as the case

may be, in accordance with the wishes of a majority of the delegation.

3. In the case of an equality of votes within the delegation in respect of any matter under consideration the leader shall have a second or casting vote.

11. Services for members and party groups

11.1   Accommodation will be provided for members on a basis to be determined by the Parliamentary and Organisation Committee, after consultation with the party leaders.

11.2   Secretarial and administrative services will be made available to the Chairman and Leader of the Council and to the leaders of other party groups and, if resources allow, to other members.

11.3   Any request for the development of the services for members will be referred to the Parliamentary and Organisation Committee after consultation with the party leaders.

11.4   Reprographic services will be provided for the use of party groups by the County Secretariat subject to the availability of resources, at a cost to be determined from time to time by the Parliamentary and Organisation Committee.

12. Press statements and relations with the media

12.1   Official press statements arising out of Council business will be made with the agreement of the chairman of the Council or committee in consultation with other party leaders or spokesman as appropriate. They will indicate whether any party group did not support the decision concerned.

12.2   The relevant party spokesmen will be sent a copy of press statements immediately they are published, and will have the right to issue a separate statement under 12.4 below.

12.3   Where a committee decision is carried against the chairman's party group, the spokesmen of the party group or groups representing the majority on that occasion will have the right to involvement in the preparation of any official press statement issued in relation to that decision.

12.4   Press statements arising out of council business issued in a party capacity by the leader or spokesman of any party may at his or her request be processed by the Public Relations and Information Officer; such press releases are published personally by the members concerned. Any costs incurred will be charged as in 11.4 to the party issuing the statement. Chief officers may be requested to provide factual information to assist in the preparation of such statements.

12.5   Chief officers may deal with any request for information or questions asked by the press, television or radio, and may accept invitations to broadcast or appear on television in order to give the facts of a situation or explain the Council's policies. Where possible the appropriate chairman and party spokesmen should be informed as soon as practicable.

13. Review

13.1   These conventions will be reviewed annually.

13.2   The Chief Executive will initiate a special review at any time if required by a change in the political balance on the Council or in the appointments of committee chairmen, or on the request of any of the parties.

APPENDICES – ACRONYMS AND LOCAL GOVERNMENT

A

AMA Association of Metropolitan Authorities
ADC Association of District Councils
ACC Association of County Councils
ALA Asociation of London Authorities
ACPO Association of Chief Police Officers
ANC Association for Neighbourhood Councils
ABCC Association of British Chambers of Commerce
ACDEPO Association of Civil Defence and Emergency Planning Officers
ACTO Association of Chief Technical Officers
ADLO Association of Direct Labour Organisations
ALC Association of Local Councillors
ADSS Association of Directors of Social Services
ADS Association of District Secretaries
ALANI Association of Local Authorities of Northern Ireland
AME Association of Municipal Engineers
Audit Commission

B

BACT British Association of Conference Towns
BASW British Association of Social Workers
BTA British Tourist Authority
BEC Builders Employers Confederation

C

CIPFA Chartered Institute of Public Finance & Accountancy
CCLGF Consultative Council for Local Government Finance
CEM Council of European Municipalities
Civic Trust
Commission for Local Administration (The Ombudsman)
CDL Consortium Developments Limited
CoSLA Convention of Scottish Local Authorities
CBI Confederation of British Industry
CPRE Commission for the Protection of Rural England
Countryside Commission

D

DiCTA District Councils Technical Association

E
ETB English Tourist Board
EHO Environmental Health Officer

F
FUMPO Federated Union of Managerial and Professional Officers

G
GWG Grant Working Group
GREA Grant Related Expenditure Assessment
GMBATU General, Municipal, Boilermakers & Allied Trades Union

H
HIP Housing Investment Programme
Housing Corporation

I
IULA International Union of Local Authorities
ILEA Inner London Education Authority
ICSA Institute of Chartered Secretaries and Administrators
IAA Institute of Administrative Accountants
ICA Institute of Chartered Accountants in England and Wales
ICMA Institute of Cost and Management Accountants
IoH Institute of Housing
INLOGOV Institute of Local Government Studies (Birmingham University)
IMBM Institute of Maintenance and Building Management
IPM Institute of Personnel Management
ITSA Institute of Trading Standards Administration
IWM Institute of Wastes Management
ICE Institution of Civil Engineers
IEHO Institution of Environmental Health Officers

J
JACOLA Joint Airports Committee of Local Authorities

L
LAMSAC
LACSAB Local Authorities Conditions of Service Advisory Board
LGORU Local Government Operational Research Unit
LGTB Local Government Training Board
LBA London Boroughs Association

M
MJ Municipal Journal
MYB Municipal Year Book

N
NALGO National and Local Government Officers Association
NALC National Association of Local Councils
NCT National Chamber of Trade
NHTPC National Housing and Town Planning Council
NJC National Joint Council
NULAS National Union of Local Authority Secretaries
NUPE National Union of Public Employees
NUT National Union of Teachers

0
OFT Office of Fair Trading
Ombudsman Commission for Local Administration
OSG Officers Steering Group

P
PTRC Planning and Transport Research and Computation Co Ltd
PWLB Public Works Loan Board

R
RSG Rate Support Grant
RWP Rates Working Party
R&VA Rating and Valuation Association
RIBA Royal Institute of British Architects
RIPA Royal Institute of Public Administration
RICS Royal Institution of Chartered Surveyors
RTPI Royal Town Planning Institute

S
SAUS School for Advanced Urban Studies (Bristol University)
SCC Scottish Consumer Council
SSHA Scottish Special Housing Association
SOLACE Society of Local Authority Chief Executives
SOCPO Society of Chief Personnel Officers
SODOPS Society of Directors of Personnel in Scotland

T
TCPA Town and Country Planning Association

W
WAA Water Authorities Association

*See Municipal Year Book for full details